DUCHESS-SIMONE ENTERTAINMENT, LLC.

A COLLECTION OF POETRY BY DUCHESS-SIMONE

CONTENTS

ACKNOWLEDGMENTS

I'd like to thank my mother, REGINA. You are my lifeline. Thank you for seeing in me a reason to live, and for holding me even when I let go of myself. If I were able to give you the world, that still wouldn't be enough. Nothing in this physical plane of existence can equate to my love, respect, and appreciation for you.

To my father, DUKE: though you are no longer in the physical realm, the warmth of your spirit makes life "bareable". Each day brings a new opportunity to make you proud. I dedicate my endeavors and ultimate success to you.

My primary school teachers, Victoria Ransome, and Maria Earl Burrell a.k.a. "Teacher Dearest"; my gratitude runs deeper than you know. Your purpose and lessons have exceeded beyond the classroom. I have carried your words of wisdom throughout my life.

And lastly, to you, reading this. From the core of my being, I appreciate you and your role in my human experience. Thank you for allowing me to impart a piece of my spirit with you, for receiving me, and for taking quite a risk in accepting the invitation to become Bare With Me. There is no turning back.

Forever Your Favorite Color,
DUCHESS-SIMONE

I, too, have phases like the moon
Bare With Me.
◗

FOUL

You
worthless
piece of shit

Sorry excuse for a man
waste of melanin
should have been swallowed
belly feeding
better off dead
worthless
piece of shit

At the bottom of the sewer
you disintegrate and rot
reminding those of your
minuscule existence

wallow in moved bowels
wallow in foul stench
darkness
is what you breathe
filth
is all you eat

grime
is all
you will ever be
I just cannot believe
God
fucking created you

So tactless
fuck the judge
I'ma hold you to your actions

A decision so senseless
"big shot" pulled the trigger
and since
your footprint's been
my necklace
for nearly two decades

Tell me how'd your freedom taste
when they failed to serve you
did you bother to say grace?
Did you bless your ribs
before your fingers felt the plate?

I'm sure for you life's been great
but for me, not exactly

I watch her day in and day out
with a face full of tears
pack us lunch and fix our meals

You ruined her life
ain't even been married a year

Tell me, "big shot"
what's your preferred
time of day?
So I know when to kick
in your door to serve you fate

I wouldn't piss or spit in a cup
to quench your dying thirst
Bow your head motherfucker
now its my turn

Don't dare hold your breath
I want your soul to seep out slow

You robbed me first
and as the story goes
you reap what you sow

You fucking coward

I'll be honest

I been dying to confront
the monster
under my bed
and hiding in my closet

You better pray
that I am either timid
forgiving
or something like my mother

cause if I turn out anything like my father
I'll show your punk ass
what it's like to be
a real nigga
and get away with murder

An Introduction

I am a P.O.E.T.
A Person
   Of
   Enlightened
   Thought
just spend some time with me
I'll have you sorting light and dark
like you're doing laundry on a breezy Sunday
life is all about choices
you can always have it your way

so babe
just tell me what you prefer
I've seen you walk the straight and narrow
but can you handle curves?
I can give you that
take you to space then bring you back
have you so
high on my frequency
like you O.D.'d on dopamine
it's rather dope of he
to notice me
in hopes that we

create the constant flow
of never ending Inner-G
that's I-n-n-e-r
capital G
gimme that O
bringing that D
ooh wee
Cause I can see that GOD power in ya

my vibe will bring it out
make you smile from within ya
please stay for awhile
let's meander in the clouds
I'll wrap you in my purple shroud
and show you how I get down

I'll put the rhythm in your rhyme
put some pep in your step
I'll help you open up your eyes
and not the physical set
your inner spirit wants to rise;
seven chakras aligned
Kundalini awakening
welcome to the divine

BLACK, MAN !

Every day's a good day to be
black, man!

Every day's a good day with a
black man!

Spread love, Give hugs,
Drink sun,
In our black land

Everyday,
Give thanks
Celebrate
'cause we black, man!

Way Back

We don't gotta be lovers
we don't even gotta be friends
But can I ask you a question
it may be a bit unrealistic
You can't promise me forever
or guarantee a couple seconds
can you reserve a little section
of your heart
in case I make my way back
Baby it's just a simple question
I'm open to the possible rejection
but it's a yes that I'm pressing
so baby tell me can I ever
try to make my way back

I'M OUT HERE

Quarter tank of gas
twenty dollars cash
negative account balance
I'm out here

No point in checking my savings
cause the checks that I'm saving
won't check for or save me
so I'm out here

Alone is what I wished for
to seek and explore
'cause I was six years old
and deprived of the world
I'm out here

Now 24 and cross country
I connect the dots to make ends meet
I'll be tracing for awhile
Clearly, I'm out here

Phoned a friend
she lent me floor space
and an air mattress

Applied for food stamps
fill the fridge as contribution
cause I can't afford rent
status updates
selfies posted with captions
"Don't worry I'm safe"
When really, I'm out here

Lied to my mama
and said I had lodging
nobody'll hire me
I'm qualified
but too vibrant
eclectic
and no lye
I'm out here

One slice peanut butter sandwiches
from the backseat
game face with a pace
like I'm gunning for first place
in a track meet

Left my ex man
he chose to marvel
at the picture as if I were a comic

Had to remind myself
it's freedom that I want
so I plant my own seeds
without a hoe I gotta harvest

I'm out here now
and won't always be 20 something
I'm out here now
I gotta figure out something
I'm out here now
and I *refuse* to be starving

I'm out here
Protective aura is my armor
In honor of my late father

I salute you Duke
promise success is my tribute

Order my words
Order my steps
Guide my verse

Because I'm out here

SELF*LESS*

Last Tuesday, a stranger
confronted me with
a personal question
"Do you want kids?"
"No." I say.

and strangely enough
Duchess became synonymous for selfish...

He told me I was selfish
for not wanting children

I said, he said, I was selfish
for not wanting children

HE TOLD ME
I was SELFISH
for not wanting fucking kids!

Never mind the fact that
I completely have the right to choose
But how dare you put a label
of ignorance might I add

on my perspective of life
With a question like,
"Don't you want to leave a legacy behind?"

Bearing in mind his level of ignorance
I decide in my reply to exhibit much gentleness

Here's my answer for that:

We can both do the math
let us pull out our pencils and pads-
Make sure your eraser is full enough
to eradicate your blunder
For you I'll break it down
and show you this work.

I am the product
of divinity multiplied by melanin
I wasn't born in sin
Unlike the sun of man
I was given a passion
to the sum of men I'm adding
Each breath I take uplifting glory

Allowing God's light to shine

Selfish you say?
I open my heart
pour out my soul

Put my life on the line
when I step up to the mic
and spit these rhymes
just for you to snap your fingers and say
"Yo she fire"

Equate that to a 9 month term
intense hours of labor
each syllable giving
birth to a nation of creators

I'm just a vessel
so I take this pain sober
Fuck the weed
Fuck the liquor
Fuck the epidural

Each time I deliver
I'm drenched in gore

Having to walk away
with my tail between my legs
Exposed and damaged

Unhealthily roaming
for the next inspiration
with hopes of another conception
of what's considered poetic perfection

I operate constantly enflamed
hoping that my purpose and name
don't die in vain
I am not selfish

I offer pieces of myself, daily.
And it's by the grace of God
that I still know what self is.

You are dismissed.

LIVE ON

my life changed
when your heart stopped beating
my tears fell without understanding
why you would not be returning
nobody really knew what to tell me
but mommy did her best at explaining
so
i tried my best to be a normal child
normal didn't get me many friends
i always imagined happier times
all the ways i wish it didn't have to end
dreams were the only way you could reach me
i taught myself how to dream awake
i even convinced myself that the bright stars
meant you were listening
i even wrote you letters
i even wrote you songs
i even wrote you poems
i wanted you so badly to know
you were still in my thoughts
i
dreamed of times i made you proud

after that time i beat you in chess
after mastering the bunny ear technique
after balancing for five minutes straight
without training wheels
after the one report card of mine that you signed
I got straight A's that time
i
wasn't afraid of spiders, heights, or ferocious beasts
my only fear was conquered when you left me
i was too young to comprehend
how your absence was a detriment
....and then i began to peak in development
what a hell i was living in
alienated
misunderstood
disadvantaged
worthless
desperate
for the hug
and the love that
i would never get
your unexpected departure had me on edge

the day you ascended
you left with pieces of me
i don't remember your voice
but your energy is familiar and unmatched
helping me to become the woman i am today
nothing can take the place of giving me your name
im ever so thankful
so many predicted my life would be different
human ignorance speaks rest in peace
but your legacy lives
I am you
I am your legacy
You live through me

LOST Herself

I see this woman,
and she looks familiar.
I admire her smile, her wit, her style,
her color-

she's just plain cool to me.
Her energy is a light tower
for those in need.

I watch how they gravitate towards her
like moths to lantern,
she guides the way
but despite providing
guidance to her cohort
She
is lost
herself.

I didn't speak for weeks
I hit my face then I hid my face for peace
Bare With Me.
◑

DIE II LOVE

I said that I was willing to die for you
But I trusted
you wouldn't be
the cause of my death
I trusted
you wouldn't push
me over the edge
I trusted
we'd maintain
a form of respect

I said that I was willing to cry for you
Guess that must have went
right over your head
'Cause you look thru
and past the overflow,
the inlets form
My spirit unfulfilled
because now I regret

though I gave my all, my best

And for each dying tear
that I have shed
I'm pleased to have died
a beautiful death

We laid in the bed
while limbs were spread
the more you gave
the more I begged

Through you, I still feel
through you, I continue
to experience the deadliest,
loving-est, saltiest tears

as you mourn my death
in the arms of another

dear friend

I stumbled upon a piece of my heart
Unexpectedly
I walked into a house
at the top of the hill
whose doors are never locked

I was greeted by familiar smiles
refreshing vibes
and that part of me
I never realize departed

Slightly taken aback
beaming uncontrollably
yet within myself
slowly but surely
the ego is folded
to be left to the left of the sofa

With nature as the fragrance
that permeates the scope
of this haven

I inhale, breathe love, find solace

Forgiveness is granted
for crimes and trespasses
intended to be carried to the grave

I relinquish

The Philly in me wishes to resist
I squelch the flame of apprehension
in dire need to break habits
I gently sit beside the ego

This time wearing the smile
once bottled up inside

To think I almost sacrificed acceptance
On the highest level
Protection of a father
Counsel of an elder
Love of a brother
Passion of a lover
In the form of a friend

A very dear friend indeed

pour me.

you speak things
I never mentioned
you fulfill my silent wishes
feels like I'm high
above clouds
I could get used to this

laying in this space
my fears nonexistent
appearing in the sky
our energy - electric

this is not to be called romance

it's been a while
since I've loved
but since I really
care for you
and the glass is half full

I'll just
go ahead
and
pour
a little me
into
you

madrugada

The Moon has finally set
Yes, we made the Sun rise
thus, we've made God smile

You, the seed
The Creator's original recipe
bury yourself in me
and we together build humanity

You don't have to wait
with power in me
harvesting season is never ending
we, together move
generate electricity

What they consider a storm
is a normal day in the life
of love to us

Your smile cuts through
8 layers of grey
thick layers of day
and shines

You, my Sun
shine bright today
and brighter than the day before
Plant one on me
before the rain again comes

My Type,

I live for that
don't mind us type of love
Earth is ours, so there's no such thing
as "in private" type of love
No need to be modest
let's behave our wildest type of love
Show up and set the climate
ringing sirens type of love
Vacation in your mind
cause we're in alignment
Never denying
forever supplying that
Type of love,
Your Favorite Color

Own Dough

Post coitus, my partner rolled over
and his words were
"Baby, you tryna bake some bread how my mama
used to do for daddy?"
Preserving my high, forced shut my eyes
But again he said, this time involving
unnecessary physical contact-
"Baaaby, can you bake bread like my mama
did for daddy?"
Rising to my feet,
applying the deadliest stare,
hoping looks could kill. Again-
"Honey, can you please bake the bread how mama
used to do for daddy?"
Reaching for my brassiere, shoes, keys, clothes,
talking my shit as I go-
"Damn!
Did it ever occur to you that your mama made bread
from the dough that your daddy brought home?
Fuck I look like,
you think you getting a free meal too?"

I came in peace
Yet depart in pieces
Bare With Me.
◗

NAMELESS

You were my greatest lesson
and no I don't regret it
my good karma's manifesting
no more needing Excedrin

I've got the best expression
realize it's such a blessing
I wake up smiling
it's been a while
Since I've done things for myself

Cause in reality
I carried us
but never held that over you
it was the cards that were dealt
but I traded my Ace
for a King
then a Queen
Nobody placed above myself
and now you know just what that means

Unless you propose a title and a ring

Baby, you are not entitled
you, don't deserve anything
you, deserve nothing

So I won't ever paint a picture
just using any colors
these hues are true
defining you
and the shade of your character
act like this never mattered
I wonder what's the matter

Cause these people thinking for you
now they speaking for you too?
I guess.

They're pulling on your heart strings
and playing puppet master

But I was never good enough
ain't go beneath my standards

The pedestal was too high
So you stayed where it was comfortable

but then you made it seem like
you wasn't even *asked* to go
you were not even *down* to go
I begged you and I pleaded
I was everything you needed
but you wanted what was easy

I expected you to rise up
and go above
what you see in your immediate
but it was just
too much for you to stomach
the cord was still attached
and mere thought of the severance

caused anxiety attacks

So I received the lash out
and then I became assed out
I put my dreams
before the one I love
and now I'm the sell out?!

Well,
fuck it 'til I cash out
won't drink until I pass out
I want to be conscious when
come time they call my name out

They'll say
"Duchie you're a star!
Tell them who you'd like to thank!"
then I'll say
"Shout out to my inspiration
nah, he don't need no name."

SEE THE TRUTH

You were it all
the center of my universe
But it seems your role
just a script well rehearsed.
You learned it well
formed a well, only sought
me when you thirst.

You didn't make a sound
your feet ain't touch the ground.
Angel,
what entity could you be serving?
One of good or one of evil.
Joy you once brought now
I wince in pain upon
hearing your name.

Internally I bleed &
I pack the wounds:
O.G, Xanies, and 70 proof.

Mind discussions 'bout loving you,
mild discussions 'bout wanting you.

Next moment I'm cussing
I'm nothing
then once again, hating you.

Can this be my reality?
Hurting deep within the fallacies.
No longer blind to see
the injustice done to me.

Your eyes ain't open.
They can't be,
because you didn't see me
or what's left of me.

But what's my excuse?
all five wide shut
and don't see the truth.

You're only capable of giving
one type of love
within a dimension in which
I'm not familiar.
I don't speak that language.

Nothing wrong with what
you gave it just wasn't enough.
Somewhere I forgot
I was raised
fed, and bred from real love
but on me you pulled a fast one.

In the air
we discovered the rushing
pleasures that adorned us.
You then burned your wings
so I could keep you soaring.
Laying on my back,
I kept you floating

Made me feel you did a favor;
kept me from seeing
how I became your slave
or you my savior.

I let you have your way.

Laid awake one day
Clung to your every move
Watched you rehearse
Followed your hands as the pages turned
I discovered

Blank is the script
Absent are the words
Battered, disgusting
and empty you were

I refrain from sleep
and the curtain has closed.

SHOW YA RIGHT

He said "you rehearse your lines more than
you tell me you love me"
and I almost lose it
QUICK to get "ethnic"
I'm talkin'
eyebrow raising, neck rolling,
shoulder shrugging, finger pointing,
toe tapping, far from-deans-list-vernacular-swearing,
all flash before my eyes, in 2.5 seconds

But on the exhale, and
ever so appalled,
I say, "you met me this way,
it's just the nature of the beast
I'm not going to apologize for
putting my work first

I will not be sorry that my energy, drive, & existence
is deeply engrossed into manifesting my passions

You claimed you were willing to ride with me
and I thought you knew
you'd might riding in the back seat

But I do apologize
darling,
for creating the false pretense
that you'd be first
You are important,
but you have to be okay with the fact that
on my to-do list, you might be last

and no baby,
I don't love you any less
but my bucket list increases by the minute

I'm lerning new ways to increase my limits
I'm growing to see that I don't have many
but you do

BEEN A FIT

You take but never give
You hear but never speak
You want to get picked up
so you can save your gas

cause after all your hourly
wages are significantly less
than mine

You pay your portion to limit costs
but don't consider treating
you walk on the outside street, which
is the only thing you do right

You reach for my hand in public

Like you've earned the right to claim me
or some shit

Like you work for the title of my man
or some shit

When really you're hoping
that I fall prey to the game

But the only thing you've
managed to play was yourself

Consider this the last time

you'll see me

FULL BLOOM

I wonder how different life would be

if we actually took heed to the posts
of the memes and the quotes
because it seems that the jokes
don't really penetrate much deeper
beyond the 15 seconds
that they mean to us the most

blink twice more and it escapes
straight to your memory bank
but in short term
only to be ignited
by an occurrence
that brings you regret
but despite that you project
a presence
with a smile that's contagious

your feelings are masked
by your exploration
of new thoughts, ideas, and experiences
you've grown to a place that emits comfort

sleeping alone in the king size bed
that you and your decisions so perfectly made
this image is beautiful

hind sight is 20/20
but the view of my future
is not altered by astigmatism

I actually see it more clearly
throw some glitter on that shit
and make it more than pretty
turning negatives to positives
counting all my blessings

uplifting truth
won't make me feel less than
and neither will you
based on your perspective

the flower still blooms
whether it's sunny or raining
but weather's always beautiful
when you know where you're going

They haunt and hunt me in dreams
I'm charged for a debt, but ain't got the means
Bare With Me.
◗

Gift & Giver

My love ain't got no limits
But my tolerance does
I can't let you walk or speak over me
just because
You have a question to be answered,
I AM the answer to your question.
Yes, Woman
is the gift and giver of life.
So humble yourself
and listen.
Our balance will restore humanity.
Be all ears, baby.

PLEASE. LOVE. YOU.

I let you go

So that you can learn to love yourself

More than you love someone else.

Though someone is me

I much rather be

A stranger

Than the source of your misery.

Do yourself a favor

please,

forget

about

me.

Your Favorite Color

Please sir,
you're staring.
Do I make you feel some type of way?
The eyes race, and indicate many things
the mouth can't seem to say.

I know you wish that I could stay
unfortunately I can't.

Of course,
I know you love your girl
But it's not supposed to be the same.
The grass is much greener over there
Or so,
that's the way you make it seem

I see through
your pot of gold that's shining.
how lucky can you really be
if the rainbow
is missing *Your Favorite Color?*

One More Time
For Ol' Boy In The Back

Only met her once
but she be on your mind for months
a fleeting encounter
only to be seen again in your dreams
can't have her in real life
so you dress your wife
in her image and likeness
suggesting that she embody
that purple body like this

but not too loud.
cool and calmly collected
images for your mood
boarding the train
with vowels already
exchanged so as you
settle in on your road
to forever you
figured you might as well
paint a corner of your car
with *Your Favorite Color*
just to keep your wheels turning.

that's whack, homie.

WON'T BE ME

You can find another
she could be a model
with beautiful hair and skin
But one thing she'll be lacking
is the way to make you happy
just 'cause she won't be me
reasons:
it's in the fleekage of my melanin
and my glitter finger nails
I bet that you won't find her
if you traveled all the way to hell
there ain't another woman
who is gonna smile at you
and make your heart sing
kinda like the way I do

I bet she's a good lover
but we both can agree
that she don't love you how I did
in fact you're reminiscing
as she's down there giving head
wondering why you fucked up
'cause you know I was the shit

you loved my natural scent
and you loved my natural hair
skin feeling like shea butter
as you lay between my legs
feeling unstoppable
in the presence of a Queen
but now you fucking with them peasants
'cause you ain't fucking with me
You ain't been keeping up with me
no messages are on my screen
I chose to go through all your tweets,
I seent you running through them streets
more than likely looking for a carbon copy
but the truth is what I speak
she ain't even half of me

she ain't even a quarter
'cause in your mind you're caught up
just the mere thought of
knowing that you once fucked up
is eating away at you
I hope
the guilt swallows you whole.

BARE

Deciding to spend her time wisely

instead of remonstrating
how bad he wronged she
she invested Inner-G
into enhancing
analyzing self
and becoming clean

She offered he
a simple remedy
of pointing out the cause
while effectively
picking apart the effect to see
where the problem
could be solved

She then realizes that
she couldn't help he
approaching the situation

wearing the hat of survivor
while he waves the flag of victor

After the tumultuous engage

She divulged that he has
in fact become an after thought
Another object of affection
began to take precedence
captivating her attention
and she absolutely loves it

She, unafraid to admit
how this new found longing
keeps her up at night

Resulting in her need to detach
withdrawing her lip service
hips and hands no longer on demand

The mere sight of he
doesn't do what it used to
Not to her mind,
or her insides

With damaged pride
he inquires,

"What nigga that got you tripping?"

He doesn't realize that he'll soon be seated
since he can't stand to be corrected

To he directly:
"This ain't it
I've grown weary of trying to appease,
please, and succumb to mediocrity.
stability, purpose, and fulfillment
I need.

More than occasional
ass rubs, ginger ale,
and plate of hot wings
"What will people think?"
no longer binds me.

Time is not a factor
it's 4 years after and I'm still here
BARE

Once Bare With Me
Now I plead *Bare With Me*!

In the midsts of dissension
we are whole, but barely

We used to counter aspirations
with each others inspiration

You bit the fruit
enthralled with sensation
but couldn't handle the knowledge
bitched out to seek shelter-

Who does that?

It's facts
BARE brings you discomfort
and just so you know
my *real* BARE is best
outside the bedroom
Outta my way, I gotta show the world
I have covered up long enough
I'll bare my bones for my own
But that's language
only a kindred soul would know
I thought you knew me, but it's clear you don't.

Won Together

Left.
I took a wrong turn
trying to make things right.

Upon my return
I learned
that my union with him
was the real detour
I lost myself when I found him
I only wrote under strain
I only wrote through my pain
my voice quivered
afraid of the words
to appear on the page

I avoided the stage
feared tarnishing his name
it became clear that
I went the wrong way
down a one way street
I should have disregarded
the traffic laws
and backed out slowly
then maybe
I wouldn't have hit the dead end

panicking
I jumped off the bridge
plunging for the life of me
forgetting that my father
would treat the matter
like innocent bungee jumping

his spirit snapped me back
into his loving grace
out of harms way
onto higher ground closer to heaven
to hear his voice
reminding
me my mama didn't raise a weakling

re-calibrated my vibration
he be the compass
predicted my location
lit the path for discovery
I am my strength
and so is he
he and I are
one together
he and I
won together

greetings and welcome to my sphere.

visit www.thecolorduchess.com for more information on upcoming releases, events, and everything *Your Favorite Color*

◑

CPSIA information can be obtained
at www.ICGtesting.com
Printed in the USA
BVHW01s0745030118
504312BV00001B/49/P